BIRMINGHAM CANAL NAVIGATION
CLIFF YATES

Newton-le-Willows

Published in the United Kingdom in 2021
by The Knives Forks And Spoons Press,
51 Pipit Avenue,
Newton-le-Willows,
Merseyside,
WA12 9RG.

ISBN 978-1-912211-73-9

Copyright © Cliff Yates, 2021.

The right of Cliff Yates to be identified as the author of this work has been asserted by them in accordance with the Copyrights, Designs and Patents Act of 1988. All rights reserved. No part of this publication may be reproduced, stored in a retrieval system, transmitted in any form or by any means, electronic, photocopying, recording or otherwise, without prior permission of the publisher.

Notes and Acknowledgements

'Collapse' – Barry Flanagan exhibition, Ikon Gallery, Sept – Nov, 2019.

'Place' - Meryl McMaster, *As Immense as the Sky* and John Walker, *New Paintings*, Ikon Gallery, Dec 2019 – Feb 2020. The John Walker quotation: William Corbett (2015), https://www.alexandregallery.com/virtual-viewing-room-visiting-artists-studios

Thanks to the editors of the following publications where some of these poems first appeared: *The North, Litter, M58, Ink Sweat & Tears, Molly Bloom, New Boots and Pantisocracies: Postcards from Malthusia, One Hand Clapping, An Educated Desire: Poems for Robert Sheppard at 60*, edited by Scott Thurston (Knives, Forks and Spoons Press, 2017). 'Born in Handsworth' was previously published in *Jam* (Smith/Doorstop, 2016). 'Spitfires Were Built in Castle Bromwich' and 'Sky Blues Bus' were commissioned by The Centre for Travel Writing Studies, Nottingham Trent University; thanks to Tim Youngs. Many of these poems have been revised and are different from those versions originally published.

Contents

Birmingham Canal	5
Lifting	6
A Sheet of Miscellaneous Studies	7
Awareness Through Movement	8
It's my Birthday we go to Ledbury	9
Collapse	10
Interaction of Colour	11
Bank Holiday	12
The Ikon's Closed, it's Monday	13
Spitfires were Built in Castle Bromwich	14
Swimming Pool	16
Born in Handsworth	17
Place	18
Bridge Café	19
Red Sky Lift	20
Temple Street	21
I've Just Invented the Tai Chi Sprout Stalk Form	22
Table 9	24
5:15 p.m. February 9th. 2017	25
A Thing to Do	26
Other Times	27
Black Sabbath Bridge	28
Mode of Delivery	29
The Science of Painting	30
Sky Blues Bus	31
Dog	34

Birmingham Canal

Sunday afternoon we walked on Crickley Hill.
Every day the light is different
evening encroaching on afternoon.

Today I remembered Dad's story –
playing by the canal as a child
he fell into a lock

someone dived in and pulled him out.
When he got home they smacked him.
He could have drowned.

This happened in Birmingham
a hundred years ago.

I think they smacked him,
I might not have remembered it right;
if he was around I'd ask him.

He died when he was ten years older
than I am now.

I imagine this in black and white
and the canal water sump oil black.
Sometimes I dream in colour.
A hundred years. Birmingham.

Stand on the library roof
look out over the city.
Dad would know the names of those hills.

Cliff Yates

Lifting

Too early at the Custard Factory
for the lunch and too late for breakfast,
the towpath's closed at Broad Street, the Ikon
galleries are shut, and it doesn't look good
for our Digbeth jerry can hardware shop
but dodge between buildings
more or less opposite the bus station
for the five workmen and mini-digger
laying paving in a dream, the foreman
on his knees, smoothing sand with bare hands
in front of the thirty-foot GARAGE DOORS
brick wall and, half-way up, the blue sign
> No lifting
> over this
> building
the dark green canister, the red board –
a composition, a film set, abstract painting.
All over Brum they're laying new paving.

A Sheet of Miscellaneous Studies

And back of Birmingham Town Hall
in the Museum & Art Gallery,
Leonardo's drawings:
A Horse Divided by Lines
A Deluge, The Bones of the Hand

while in the basement, Lucy Gunning
in the red dress, still climbing
along her skirting, wardrobe,
chest of drawers, shelving, door frame

That time in Paris when you touched
the Van Gogh, sensed the paint's thickness
The Fall of Light on a Face
You'll never be that close again

Cliff Yates

Awareness Through Movement
'Without movement life is unthinkable.'
— Moshe Feldenkrais

The fish here is good, you don't have to
have it battered you can have it grilled.
I'm talking too fast, aren't I?

We're a week early for the festival
but timed it just right for the parade,
they may or may not have the horse.

It's a high ceiling and the heater's on the stage.
Your lungs go to the bottom of your rib cage,
it's easy to forget that. I'm not sure I knew.
They're three-dimensional.

I think I'm getting the hang of this
there's music rehearsing downstairs
that's not as bad as the fire alarm.

The tea tastes of bleach we buy plastic
bottles of water from the Co-op
then discover that if you run and run
the tap, it's not so bad.

You're from Okehampton
that's near Sheepwash, isn't it?
Usually it's my dad here, the boy said,
and gave us a free small lemon.

It's my Birthday we go to Ledbury

And after lunch in Chez Pascal (*I cooked
these mince pies for your birthday*)
I head back with the kids in our old Fiesta,
Luke driving: Tom Waits, Wolf Parade,
'Safe as Milk', and he gives me for my birthday

a white frisbee (why did he choose *white*?)
Discraft 175 gram Ultra Star Sport Disc
electric blue lettering that changes
colour when you tilt it. For supper, takeaway
Fat Toni pizzas, the one with the artichoke

but first we try out the frisbee on the field
before it gets dark. When Gill comes to find us
the moon's over the hill but she can still
hear our voices and see the white frisbee
flying between us catching the light.

Collapse

just a short walk
    from Paradise –

the hare's frozen leap,
insect metal, the Singer
sewing machine
in the hut, back of the lorry
mix the cement, shape it,
stitch the cloth skin
                there's rain and
wind but later it's warmer

Tell me again what she said
when you sent her your photo
of *The Heap '67 (1967)*

Everything's collapsing – not everything,
that hare won't collapse – watch it box

The post office machine spits
out your stamp and the illicit book's
sent on its way, the first three
chapters enough
                their new album
will be their best yet, no question

There were houses here
now there's money, private money
and they pay people to show people
how to use the machines

Sand in a metal bucket
sand from a hole in the sea

Interaction of Colour

There are kids on the train it's half-term, they're excited,
the two wearing cartoon tops, one drawing the other.
Going down, miming the voice of the singing lift
if you start too low there's nowhere to go.

The two pinks are different, the stripe on the wall
and where it continues on the floor. Yes,
they had to add white to get the paint right
don't tell them downstairs I said that.

We found that Josef Albers book you recommended,
it's brilliant we're going to buy a copy. Damn,
she'll think we're together. / Go back, say to her,
by the way, my wife thinks I'm crazy. / That's a good idea.

Codeine Phospate 30mg. May make you sleepy.
If this happens do not drive or use tools or machines.
Do not drink alcohol. Keep them in your suitcase
at customs. I will and I'll take my prescription, in case.

All these fried eggs, ceramic dartboards
they'd be a nightmare to live with, a nightmare.
After six weeks confined to the house, with Low
as a soundtrack, a stroll to the bus stop is something else.

We're moving into the Ikon Resource Room.
Sure, they'll make us a cuppa now and then.
The two grey armchairs to sleep on, we'll be fine.
We'll invite Rob over when he's back off his tour.

Bank Holiday

I feel like I'm part of the garden.
Did I really just say that? Yes.
She looks up from the salad.
With bits in my hair, scratches
on my arms, I'm sweating
having cut down the branches
of the lilac overhanging
the greenhouse, straining to reach
on the compost bin,
each branch the size of a tree;
there's dried blossom on the floor
in the kitchen and the hall
from where I carried through armfuls
to the garden bin out front.
Expecting a delivery, we can't eat
in the garden (we'll not hear them)
and the kitchen's too hot so we eat
in the sitting room on the settee
omelette new potatoes and salad
then watch the end of *The Homesman*
that we started last night after the cup final
(Arsenal 2 Chelsea 1),
music by Marco Beltrami (wind piano).
It's a miracle you didn't smash the greenhouse. / I know.

The Ikon's closed, it's Monday

The Ikon's closed, it's Monday.
Is Rob asleep inside and all
the girls that work there?

Here, this bend
in the canal where the lad
in the narrow boat leaned

on the tiller and nearly
hit the wall, he should be
here soon, and those two coppers

at the demo in Victoria Square
not wearing ties
will be almost grown up now.

This place will do fine
with the hiss of the steam
from the coffee machine.

Talk into the mic
reel off names like years.
He handled it right

made everything possible.
He hated football
we talked about football.

Cliff Yates

Spitfires were built in Castle Bromwich

1. Thinktank Birmingham 2019 / Aircraft factory 1940

Iconic the shape
above us, the spread
of the wings

Let's hear it for the women
of the engine production line
the lathe, the drill, the milling machine

Sit in the cut-away cockpit
pull back the lever, press
the red button
for the muffled drone

For the mechanics, riggers and fitters
assembling Spitfires in the assembly shed

Falafel sandwiches, mugs of tea
and a Penguin, all we need
as out on the street
snow turns to ice

For the sunken rivets and the elliptical wing
For the first test run –
the precision roll and the vertical climb

No grip, and we're single file
on the pavement, holding onto the rail
shouting to be heard
shouting into the cold

Panning shot of Spitfire flying at speed

2. Fisher & Ludlow, Castle Bromwich (former aircraft factory) 1950

Mum in the offices,
Dad on a job there,
carpenter and joiner.

She notices how his boots are shiny
('a man who cleans his shoes ... ')
how he's always neat and clean –

collar and tie, brown denim overalls,
pencil behind his ear –
and respectful, they're not all like that.

'Would you like to come to the dance?'
'No,' she said, 'I can't dance.'
'I can teach you.'

Cliff Yates

Swimming Pool

I thought they let the water out at night,
but no. In the glow from the security lights
it shimmers blue, a ghost of itself.
The changing rooms around the pool,
doors open, appear to wait.
I could take off my clothes and swim,
sit on the side and drip dry,
put on my clothes and dive back in.

The art deco ceiling's impossibly high,
the colours half-colours in the humid light.
I take off my shoes and socks,
walk round the pool, taste the quiet.
No echo, just the heater's hum,
the tiles cool on the soles of my feet.
A monk in cloisters, I have been here
for years, I've been here forever.

There's a clock on the wall with no hands.
It is any time and no time
                              it is that time
when we were children, me and my brother –
Dad, just in from work after his dinner
takes us to the club at West Bromwich.
He waves from the café, watches us
learn how to swim, dare to dive,
our arms stretched high above our heads.

And afterwards the crisps with the tiny blue bag,
salt on my fingers upstairs on the bus,
the lights in the shops, the streetlamps,
Dad's warmth through his overcoat,
the smell of chlorine on the back of my hands.

Born in Handsworth

My blowlamp eyes are Soho Road
that see as far as Perry Barr
my hair is Yardley Wood, my head
Barr Beacon, my gut the spiral
of Spaghetti Junction, my arteries
are the canal or maybe the Rea

The crick in my neck is Kingstanding
the Bull Ring a navel piercing
my vertebrae the Jewellery Quarter
my belly's Digbeth, my brain Five Ways
my spinal fluid's rain, just rain
on Lickey Hills, on Cannock Chase
my beating heart is Villa Park

Cliff Yates

Place

Never mind Head-Smashed-In Buffalo Jump,
looking back over your shoulder, a basket of crows,
a boat across the water with ancestors at your back;
how about our own version of 'Immense' here in Brum –
strategic selfies blown up canvas-size.

I'll carry my dad's bag of tools, wear one of his berets,
ride his old bike, wear a fairisle pullover
under brown denim overalls, and clean up my boots.
I'll pack his longest screwdriver, brace & bit, claw hammer.
Bring your camera and we'll choose our sites:
Paradise Circus, the Jewellery Quarter, Snow Hill,
Victoria Square, Gas Street, that bend in the canal

and the fisherman with the gear, forever
reeling in, dismantling his rod, setting up again
never mind the fish and the paraphernalia,
it's gazing at the float in the cold, gazing at the water.

John Walker didn't paint Seal Point when the tide was in,
he waited for the detritus, the stink.
'Tidal Change', 'Fishing with Tom and Les',
'Looking in', 'John's Bay Pollution', paint as mud:
pick up this coloured mud, he said, *and turn it into air.*
Stripes, zigzags and fish, Aboriginal bark painting,
his dad in Passchendaele, World War 1.
Where there aren't any footprints, you make your own.

Bridge Café

Three teapots between us, one for hot water,
white enamel, grey, and the red –
if we stole two, we'd leave them the red.

The Gas Hall shut between exhibitions –
next it's Fifty Years of Black Sabbath,
twelve quid and booking compulsory, a joke

they demolished back-to-backs
to build Corporation Street
and no record of what people said.

Carhartt cap and Carhartt trousers,
you're a walking advert.   I know,
and neither of us have an umbrella.

Saturday it's Eurostar but tonight
it's the family bag of crisps, the plateful of rice
and snooker on the telly, and remember –

buildings hold memories, like our place –
paint the walls, move the furniture, start over.
'You *were* always chewing, I remember.'

Red Sky Lift

It's lunchtime just forty minutes so I take
the stairs, not wait for the lift and head out
through the automatic doors into the winter sunshine.
In the Students' Union I check out the headlines
and buy a Twix: *I haven't bought one of these
for twenty years,* I say to the woman
behind the counter. *Well don't wait twenty
before the next one,* she says. It's more like
forty, I realise, unwrapping it – morning break
in the printing factory, something
to look forward to, like 'Mr Fantasy'
on the turntable or Quicksilver
Messenger Service.
                      I cut across to the Doug
Ellis Sports Centre and the art deco swimming pool.
I rarely go swimming but there's something relaxing
about the smell of chlorine, the stretch of blue
under those massive beams, the slow lane
and the slower lane, the lifeguard
in her red tracksuit.
                   The Twix half gone,
I head for the library for a takeaway decaf,
then back in the Main Building the red sky lift
is on its way down for once, and only five
of us waiting we'll easily fit in.

Temple Street

On Temple Street, a lad
with no shoes in grey socks hands over
a lighted cigarette without stopping

or looking to the girl with the pony tail
selling The Big Issue,
her belongings and dog beside her

near the cathedral
where you remembered
the grounds full of starlings.

Thought I saw you on Corporation Street
yesterday – in your early fifties,
wearing that raincoat, climbing on a bus.

Cliff Yates

I've Just Invented the Tai Chi Sprout Stalk Form

Boxing Day and I'm in the garden
practising the Tai Chi Spear Form
with the curtain pole that Andy found
for me in the tip. The kids are watching
through the window over breakfast.
I'm just doing the final moves:
    Bright Rainbow Soaring to the Sun
    Lying Tiger Diving Dragon
    Plum Blossom Opens Five Petals
    Celestial Horse Walks the Skies
when Luke opens the back door
and lobs the sprout stalk at my head.
Watch out, Dad, he says. I rescue
the sprout stalk from the fig tree
and spontaneously invent and perform,
there and then, the Tai Chi Sprout Stalk Form.
I even have names for the moves:
    Beginning Style
    Wet Dishcloth Wings Through Damp Air
    Dustbin Lid Exits Coal Bunker at Speed
    Rocking Chair Becomes Disagreeable
    Bag of Flour Explodes at Bus Stop, there are Casualties
    Rubber Ball Bounces in Dark Subway
    Sash Window Slams Shut on Ring Finger
    Coat Hanger Attacks Privet Hedge
    Windmill Plays Saxophone in High Wind
    Banana Smashes Pineapple on Lino
    Telephone Wires Entangle in Radio Waves
    Ironing Board Makes Sandwich with Secret Ingredient
    Public Library Saves City from Avalanche
    Sherbet Fountain Takes Umbrage and Spins
    Warehouse Fills Sky, Sky Exacts Revenge
    Helicopter Hovers Over Sycamore
    Dual Carriageway Gets Up and Walks

Kettle's boiled, Dad! / OK, thanks.
I throw the sprout stalk back into the fig tree
(Completion Style). Now, breakfast.

Table 9

Table 9 in The Kanteen
Frankie the boxer
shows his teeth and doesn't mean it

Toasted kofta baguette,
carrot cake & a pot of tea
opposite The Greenhouse

Drops of rain, faster now
on the water feature
You can't judge by experiences

What is there, here? she says,
I know what there used to be

A man carrying pink
carnations in a black plastic bucket
on the spiral staircase

It used to be the Custard Factory / I know

and just a short walk away
the angel suspended life-size
floating feet down above the flowers
a star in both hands

5:15 p.m. February 9th. 2017
i.m. Tom Raworth and after 'Wedding Day'

      the night he rang me
from a pay phone in Chicago
during an ice storm

        & that time in Robert's
office before the reading by the radiator too hot to touch
patiently signing my stack of his books:

for Cliff
    after dinner –
– before filing cabinet
        with good wishes
            Tom
  Edge Hill – February 15th 2001

& on the train from Watford Junction, shivering
in air conditioning
      the couple opposite might've slept
in their clothes   a flower

in his buttonhole, her hat,
his jacket round her, her head on his
shoulder &
      I was very impressed,
she said, *with how much*
they enjoyed their wedding day

Cliff Yates

A Thing to Do

In the midst of a family crisis
seemingly unending and unsolvable
the only book I'm able to read
is Roy Fisher's *Slakki*,
the same handful of poems
over and over.
I almost understand them.

Other Times
for Robert Sheppard

'Did you see the cat on your travels?'
'I saw the sky, blue and raring to go, I saw a red bus NOT IN SERVICE going at walking pace on the ring road ... '
'We're so lucky when you think about it. How long's it been, since the ceasefire?'
'I've been checking out that leak in the bedroom. I think I might be onto something.'
'Do you have to wear that old hat in the house? It's not as if we have no money.'
'We need to take down the curtains, have a really good look.'
'I'll help you when I've finished this. I'm so happy, it's almost like the old days.'

* * *

'Have you seen my sunglasses?'
'Why, who are you trying to impress?'
'That's the second time you've asked me that.'
'Sunglasses are just curtains. Light is to be welcomed, like the absence of a sore throat.'
'I have a sore throat therefore I need sunglasses, have you seen my sunglasses? I thought they were in the kitchen ... '
'But you can't find them in the kitchen. Water in the kettle, in the aquarium, all we need when we turn on the tap and still ... '
'It pours and pours like the end of the world. There's a gap in the skirting. I keep noticing it, in the bathroom opposite the bath.'
'I can't imagine not living here. I know my way about with my eyes closed.'
'Everyone heads south for the winter, whether or not they leave the house.'

Black Sabbath Bridge

on Broad Street, with a plaque
calling them a *Birmingham export*.
But what did Birmingham actually *think*
of Black Sabbath, back then?
For instance, I had long hair
which had only recently been invented
and in Brum one day with Enzo
I decided to call in and see Uncle Fred,
remembering he worked in Greys –
hadn't seen him for years.

When the lift doors open, he's there
with his mates in brown overalls
like Dad's, a pencil behind his ear
and he looks at me
and I don't know what to say.

You went to see Fred, Mum says,
what – looking like that?

Steve bought their first album.
We played it on the portable record player
in the barn after band practice
rehearsing for a gig that didn't materialise.
What – looking like that?

Mode of Delivery
for Andrew Taylor

You've given up chocolate for Lent
and I have a brownie and hot chocolate

surface is good if there's stuff going on
the one with the red has more depth

compare it with getting up
and not getting dressed

they don't come close to the John Salt
and that was way back

Cliff Yates

The Science of Painting

On the 20.31 Eurostar from St Pancras
we share the family bag of cheese & onion

'Mixing Colours' on my phone
Shackleton's Malt in your hip flask

2am knackered, it's worth it and more
for the Leonardo in the Louvre –

the security guard yawning in the corner
extra Madeleines for the journey home

we're a long way from the Custard Factory
Gare du Nord is not New Street

the Louvre isn't the Ikon and even though
it's February, it's way too hot

in the crowds, in our winter coats
queuing for the Virgin of the Rocks

Sky Blues Bus

1. 17th May 1987 [in the voice of a 1980s BBC newsreader]

On a historic day in the Midlands,
PDU 125M, the last bus to be built
in Coventry, this morning
carried Coventry City football team
on their victory parade through the city,
following their 3-2 defeat
of Tottenham Hotspur
in yesterday's FA cup final.

The Daimler Fleetline, donated
to Coventry Transport Museum
just last year, was painted sky blue
and converted to an open top vehicle
specially for the parade.

Asked for a statement, after
what will most likely be
its last journey anywhere,
the bus was reportedly too choked
with emotion to be able to speak.

A lifelong Coventry City supporter,
this was undoubtedly
the proudest moment of its working life.

2. The impact of the Coventry bombing
on the city's transport infrastructure

My mother in Hall Green, Birmingham,
lying in bed, 14 November 1940
after her shift in the factory (toolmaker)
hearing the planes flying over, one after the other
and the relentless, night-long sound of bombs:
'I remember thinking, somebody's getting it.'

Salvage from the tramway tracks was enough
to build 180 heavy tanks, but the Coventry bombing
did it for the trams.   An abandoned tram
found in a garden, blown over the house in the night,
windows intact.

3. 17th May 1987: The last bus

Sky blue flags and sky-blue scarves
people on a roof, hanging out of windows
climbed up traffic lights, climbed up trees
    cheering for the players
    cheering for their team
    cheering for the victory
    cheering for the dream
their heroes waving, smiling, holding up the cup
on the open top deck of the double decker bus

Apart from the bus route, the streets are quiet
ghost town
Sunday
listen –
turn down the volume of the shouting and the singing
listen –
underneath the shouting
underneath the singing
the bus is in a dream …

They're cheering me on, cheering me on
they're cheering on the last bus home
    there's no blues like the sky blues
cheering on the last bus home

Cliff Yates

Dog

So many places closed: the off-licence,
the butcher, the corner shop, even
the telephone box screwed shut.
Dog had come a long way, and now what?

The cherry blossom, he noted,
looking up for once from the pavement,
was particularly stunning this year,
maybe it was the same every year

but noticing it, his heart was lifted
and he decided not to be disappointed.
The journey had been arduous, the future
was uncertain, but there is more to life,

he reflected, cocking his leg against the letter box,
than a bowl of fruit on a table.

www.ingramcontent.com/pod-product-compliance
Lightning Source LLC
Chambersburg PA
CBHW011957060426
42444CB00046B/3459